Random Music in a Small Galaxy

Random Music in a Small Galaxy

Poems by

Margot Wizansky

© 2025 Margot Wizansky. All rights reserved.
This material may not be reproduced in any form, published,
reprinted, recorded, performed, broadcast,
rewritten, or redistributed without
the explicit permission of Margot Wizansky.
All such actions are strictly prohibited by law.

Cover design by Sasha Wizansky
Cover image "Beach at Lincoln City, Oregon"
by Margot Wizansky
Author photo by David Wizansky

ISBN: 978-1-63980-751-2

Kelsay Books
502 South 1040 East, A-119
American Fork, Utah 84003
Kelsaybooks.com

to my poetry community, which keeps me going

Acknowledgments

I acknowledge, with gratitude, the editors of these journals and anthologies where a number of these poems were published previously, sometimes in different versions with different titles.

American Literary Review: "Soldier" as "Dirge for the Artist"
The Antigonish Review, Kalliope: "Sweetie, Sweetie"
Boston Herald: "Would Anything Have Been Different?" as "If the Mothers," "Sweetie, Sweetie"
The Cancer Poetry Project 2: "Sweetie, Sweetie"
Chester H. Jones Foundation National Poetry Competition Winners Collection: "To Swim with Dolphins"
Consequence: "Keep Marching" as "Leaving Auschwitz, January, 1945," "The Lost Children," "Migrating Ducks Make Me Think of Nazis"
Crab Orchard Review: "Southwestern"
Exit 7: "Before There Were Women," "On a Barren Plain" as "The Plain of Mysteries"
Grief and the Healing Arts: Creativity as Therapy: "On Good Friday" as "Esperanza"
The Ibbetson Review: "Sweetie, Sweetie"
Lily Poetry Review: "The Reign of Her Dying"
Mercy of Tides: Poems for a Beach House: "To Swim with Dolphins"
Potomac Review: "The Burqa" as "Still Life with Pomegranate"
Quarterly West: "Midwife"
Sanctuary: "Voyeur" as "Ephemera"
The Senior Times: "On Good Friday" as "Esperanza," "To Swim with Dolphins"
swifts & slows: "When I Kneel Down," "Backlash," "After the Oil Spill, the Loons"
Voices from the Attic: "Toehold"
WCAI Poetry Sunday: "Before There Were Women

Contents

One

Before There Were Women	17
Indifference	18
On a Barren Plain	19
The Purpose of Dung	20
In the Copper Canyon, a Sheer Drop into Wildness	21
When I Kneel Down	23
Voyeur	24
Lost	25
On Reading Psalm 15	26
Answering the 23rd	27
Weather	28

Two

To the Astonishment of Creation, Here Confined	31
Backlash	32
In Trout River, Newfoundland	33
The Biologist Dissects a Sperm Whale, Beached on the North Sea	34
Whale Hunt in the Grenadines	35
After the Oil Spill, the Loons	36
Two Donkeys in Doolin, Ireland	37
Kris Feeds the Animals	38
Ode to the Oysters	39
How to Become a Naturalist	41

Three

Nor'easter, Salty Cottage	45
My Feet Are Planted on this Rock	46
Water	48
A Small Caribbean Island with a Line from Auden	49
Night Hisses Its Fast Downpour	50
The Green of Ireland	51
Independence	53
Southwestern	54
Ode to Cidering	55

Four 57

Winter Never Came	59
The Constant Stream	60
Would Anything Have Been Different?	61
The Burqa	62
The Birds in Babylon	64
The Lost Children	66
Earthquake Artists	67
Migrating Ducks	68
A Polish Woman, About to Save a Jewish Child Hiding Under Her Church Pew, Hesitates	69
Intimacy	70
Keep Marching	71
Soldier	72
Five Ways of Spoons	73

Five

The Application of Luck 77
To Swim with Dolphins 78
On Good Friday 79
The Reign of Her Dying 80
Sweetie, Sweetie 81
Midwife 83
Refugees 85
Citizenship 86
Toehold 88
Random Music 89

The universe in fact is monstrously indifferent to the presence of man / We are small as moth wing fall / in an orchestra broad as galaxies / playing a symphony Time isn't bothered to fathom / it respects no constant and is always moving on

—Inua Ellams

One

Before There Were Women

Men knew nothing of the seasons of water.
They did not bathe in the river nor catch rain
in their mouths. Neither did they quarry
nor plant nor build. They had no plans,

wandered aimless as a line without a hook
until the god of forethought
stole for them the wherewithal,
all the fiery arts and comforts—

rings and anklets of precious metal,
goblets blown from molten glass,
grilles for their meats,
and they took their pleasure and were not

entangled in the weedy glen of longing.
Then women made their entrance,
fluttering in silk, herb-scented,
and strapped men onto the rack of desire.

And the one whose hair was twined
with mimosa bore gifts, and she flung
the box open and spread calamity—
insanity, misery with no voice,

the human inability to match effect with cause,
the hopeless inconstancy of passion,
and so delivered us our cursed narrative—
the history of love.

Indifference

County Sligo, Ireland

The great stones knew weightlessness,
they balanced on a fulcrum, pivoted
their very existence uphill, depending
on the heave to the mountaintop,
lined up by season, mid-season,
by the dominant hills, by the strongest sun,
a landscape of stones: slabs and corbels,
a gallery, a grave for the queen
who conquered the king,
and a granite capstone.
The stones spoke, a trick
of hollowing the surface
to catch the wind's percussion.
The people heard the voice in their heads
and a keening in their bones.
They were afraid and paid homage,
the masses of men who labored
to build one mound, who didn't
know old age, slept longest
in the dark months, fractured
before the work was done.
The stones had nothing to do
with remembering them, laid out
where they fell on the lower slopes.
Stone over stone the years tolled,
indifferent to the toil of men
keeping the sun in its place.

On a Barren Plain

Thingvellir Rift, Iceland

You're dying to see the rift, so we
drive all day in pounding rain,
hail, blue mist. Plumes of steam.
Depressions of impossibly neon waters.
Banks of sulphur-yellow moss. Rocks, lava.
Horses in their desultory huddle
nosing and humping. Only one billboard
rises up in front of us. Embossed
in two languages: *Thingvellir Park.
Enter Here.* And beyond the sign,
no entrance, no gate. The road
stretches on in barrenness. Time
is made not of hours, not of day, not night.
Time is nothing to be marked.
100,000 years a fissure widening enough
for a stone-wheeled cart to rumble through.
We stand in that shallow crevasse, you,
enthralled to be in the rift.
I'd expected earth's thundering,
bells, an ushering in—earth, rupturing,
and we, the only witnesses.
On our map it's a simple jagged line.

The Purpose of Dung

In the Grand Canyon,
a mule train descends. I press
against the strata as it passes,
the trail paved with dung,
the hanging reek of it. Swallows
plunder the shimmering mounds,

clack and pick what they need.
They ignore me in their busyness
though I'm inches away.
They whirl and soar to the rim,
scattering wildflowers
with their droppings, a carpet

of miniature lupines,
each blossom a small steeple
of blue—an infinitesimal event
in the canyon's grand scale—
from mules to birds—
from dung to blessèd dung.

In the Copper Canyon, a Sheer Drop into Wildness

Batopilas, Mexico

Here, the canyon's a slit in the earth's surface and everything
the canyon people know of light and dark is contained within.
Very few of us tourists. On New Year's Eve the locals dress up
to dance in the Zocalo, the girls bare-armed in sequined gowns,

every man wearing the same stiff black cowboy hat. The night
is very cold. I sit on a park bench next to a woman, warmed
by her body heat. We feel unseen. This isn't our party.
At midnight, the crowd runs to the cathedral. We follow.

Everyone prays to the Black Madonna. Back at our hotel,
rifle shots ring out just below our window and repeat,
frightening until we realize they're celebratory. One day we hike
a dirt path to a little outpost, directions from a guide we met

at breakfast—*follow the dry streambed, turn at the rock pile.*
The path begins along the river. The water's milky. As we climb
away from the river, everything looks the same—dust, white-
hotness, crumbling footholds, bone-dry streambeds.

We might be lost. Over peanut butter and crackers, we reconnoiter
when a mustachioed man rides up on an enormous horse, asks if
we're looking for Bahuichivo, which we are. He motions us to
follow and eventually we enter a clearing, an immaculate barnyard

raked until the dirt ripples like water, a donkey grazing,
a few chickens scrabbling, a family who welcomes us, leads us
through stands of giant elephant cactus to the canyon's ridge.
As if all footpaths converge here to behold earth's ancient

underpinnings—six copper canyons, every canyon carved by
water, six rivers merge and split again, millions of years
of matter, fractured brilliance of verdigris and bronze, adamant sky,
the way it was as creation hardened magma, as it is still,
holy time exposed.

When I Kneel Down

The Tablelands, Gros Morne, Newfoundland

The mantle, heaved up six hundred
million years ago. Or five hundred million,
millions dropped, just like that.

A small stone weighs much more
than I expected, heavy metal,
iron and chromium, toxic, inhospitable.

Yet, when I kneel down, here is moss,
alive in a bit of dirt caught by wind.
Grey grasses, poking through, wait for

a few drops of rain to turn green.
Junipers grow flat, trunks keeping
to the ground. And flowers—

the pitcher plant's flute-full
of insects, and the tiniest allium,
flushed, abiding.

Voyeur

Just as the raspberries reach
their fragile fullness, and I've
armored myself, leather-gloved,
to pick among thorns, the wasps
beat me to them. I'm a voyeur—
the way the wasps take the berries—
each wasp a little cameo on deep red,
sucking the drupelets, juices dripping,
berry disintegrating—brazen feast!
It aches with beauty, this momentary
life, whether or not we use it well.
It plays us, like that old joke on me:
gift-wrapped box after box,
ribboned and glittered, nested
one inside the other, all empty,
even the last box—only the world
dangling before me, sparkling fine.

Lost

> *a little lower than the angels . . .*
> —Psalm 8

Beneath the great spill of moon and stars,
the steady hum of technology drowns out

the barred owl's cry and the utter quiet
that lets us hear our body-sounds,

heart's pulse, blood's gurgle. Unnatural light
obscures the one-celled life

that glowed in Mosquito Bay. Great whales
starve, as do their sucklings, whatsoever passes

through the paths of the sea. We dismiss
the dark, trade sleep for constant screens.

We shatter the certainty of home,
make refugees of millions. Wetlands we call

swamps, and drain them. A little lower
than angels, we pick our way around

garbage in the harbors. The gyre threatens
to engulf us. We forgot our time here

is provisional and ownership, finite.
We used to study glory.

On Reading Psalm 15

Forgive God
For being only a word
　　　—Mark Jarman

I can't ask God to fix my life.
It's deep winter and I long
for the coming of curling ferns.
Cry all I want—God won't hear me.
Pray, but prayer is insignificant,
less than nothing on the wind.
People insist on a God who is there,
like a little man. He can't shield us from
our enemies. No one's in the tabernacle,
and liars move freely. Borrowers
suffer, lenders reap a mighty profit,
fear no retribution. We ought
to know from the psalms, praising
God won't save us. Plant your tree,
meditate on the Lord day and night.
The leaf will still wither from dryness
and heat. We should get credit
ourselves when the corn increases.
Let us turn to our children for peace,
their warm, unconditional arms.

Answering the 23rd

Surely goodness and mercy shall follow me . . .
                                            —Psalm 23

1
I am my own shepherd. I am guilty of too much wanting.

2
I don't lie down in green pastures. I don't go near still waters
where parasites lurk.

3
We were born with our souls arisen, starry and pure.
The most beautiful paths meander.

4
We walk toward our deaths every day, like a blind-folded donkey
collared to the grinding-stone, picking our way through evils
unimaginable in Jehovah time: rods and staffs,
simply other forms of weaponry.

5
I prepare my own table to dine among friends
who need not anoint me; I provide the oil, pour the wine,
let my loving overflow.

6
My father, a good man, died so young;
surely mercilessness has followed me all the days of my life,
and has made me fear every twinge of my heart.

Weather

We are accounted as sheep for the slaughter . . .
—Psalm 44

Praise God, said our forefathers, and we did,
never forgetting, never mis-stepping.
God isn't enriched by selling His people,
yet He has given us up like sheep intended for food.
The city was once spice and sweetness,
and music filled the corners. The light is gone.
Rain fills all the buckets, and we abandon
our houses, weeping, climb to the roof
to wait for rescue. Dogs and grandmothers
float by, tiring. We can't fight the wrath
of His weather, coming in like the shadow
of death, the storm, a dragon disguised. Still,
we go on singing in the shelters, praising God
who has scattered us and confused us.

Two

To the Astonishment of Creation, Here Confined

Three elephants in the zoo, in a
tiny cage that holds their exact
dimensions, three walls, a row of
bars, their half-lives drawn into
themselves, their eyes deep-sunk
in the insult this hobbled room
allots them. The keeper offers a
bright blue circus ball. Now and
then one of the elephants bats it
about with its trunk, raises a dust
cloud from the dry straw on the
floor. Whenever one steps, two
others must also step. When one
turns, three turn. Massive, weight-
less, they move as a single being.
I could call it a dance, the way
they inhabit this shoddy space, but
it's so much more. In the dim, their
wrinkles turn velvet. A shaft of sun
gives their heads an unearthly glow.

Backlash

In Newfoundland, the constancy
of fog. Thousands upon thousands
of pelagic birds share the sea stacks

in the stink—murres protect their eggs
on the narrowest ledge, gannets plunge-dive, raucous,
gulls food-snatch, egg-snatch.

Puffin pairs fail to hatch one egg,
launch one chick. Whales are thrown off course
searching for food, polar bears wander through town.

Baby seals throw themselves on Twillingate Beach to die.
A campaign was mounted to save them. That ancient hunt
forbidden, they multiply and multiply,

eat and eat. The more we save, the more die
of starvation. A hurricane topples
the massive rig looking for oil in the sea.

In Trout River, Newfoundland

The capelin are rolling,
though I don't know
anything about capelin.
I should have asked.
Are they alive when
you take them in your bucket
from the sand? Alive
when you fry them? Or
do you cut their heads off?
Take out their guts?
Do they have bones that
could stick in my throat?
The capelin are rolling,
spawning and rolling
on the beach to die.
They have to die.
Their silvery bodies
turning pink with early rot,
the surface of the sea like
"The Triumph of Death,"
tranquil from afar,
but close-up, utter chaos.

The Biologist Dissects a Sperm Whale, Beached on the North Sea

She extracts a tooth
that fit in the marvelous maw
like a pin in a socket, slices through
layers still fresh as the butcher's aisle,
alabaster fat, a lacery of veins, hinged ribs
that narrowed the head for diving. She cuts a
passage to the blowhole, nostril that beat breath
to song, and deep inside, lips, those black monkey
lips that clicked in codas, the voice box big as she is.
All day she works to cut a window to the heart, three
empty stomachs, door into carnage. She ducks the gassy
spew, bags up an extravagance of bowel. Spermaceti
pours from the head, waste of oil the Union would
battle for, spilling down the flanks, skin sucker-scarred
from giant squid, tail, propeller of every plunge and
rise, small slit of anus. The ancient hooded stare
of eye, and fifty feet away, she hunkers in the
muck, leans on his barnacled side, draws
the penis, gleaming, out of its sheath,
indigo blue, satiny, curled inside
for years until a female gave
it entry, lapping now at
incoming tide, longer
than she is tall,
thick as her arm.
Prehensile. She
drapes it across
her lap, flings it
back and forth to show
the measure of flex and coil,
gives praise to his   angles of thrust,
cetaceous, and belly   to belly, like us, and
fifteen showers later,   she still smells of whale.

Whale Hunt in the Grenadines

The whaleboat, a small fresh-painted boat,
and a six-man crew with nothing to lose
but the unbridled daring they're heir to
and broken boats drowned by angry whales.

They go for the legal kill.
Mother and calf, count one.

The lookout shouts *Whale!* The first mate,
in a mirror-flash hoists sail for the chase.
Close enough, the harpoonist hurls
wood to black skin and the whale
takes it running unto exhaustion.
Then all the crewmen plunge their lances in,
fifty lances deep. A fountain!
All night they wait through the long slow dying.

Dawn, they lash it tight to the boat and the stitcher
climbs its back, sews its mouth closed. They tow it home
for the butchering. Islanders come, wading into the bloody sea.

The tourists turn in disgust.

These are old ways, not written but told,
grandfather to father, father to son.
The gates of their houses are ribs of whale.

After the Oil Spill, the Loons

They're hardest to wash. How tenuous
they are, black and matted, intricate
barbules in disarray, dotted breasts gummed

with the black of greed. We feed them
a slurry, fill eight basins, the first,
pure liquid soap, the second, diluted

with a little water, and so on, until
the last basin, clear and warm.
In the first basin, we hold one by the legs

while we scrub its body, swab its eyes,
trying not to scare it. We move it to
the second basin and slowly down the line.

They tremble. We hear none of their
tremolo or wail. They try to hide
their heads under their wings.

In a wading pool protected by mesh,
we encourage them to preen.
Without their natural oils, they drown.

Most of them we lose anyway,
        no matter how careful we are,
                how quiet.

Two Donkeys in Doolin, Ireland

As though one would die
without touching the other,
they bump and nuzzle, nose to neck,

Hundreds of years they've been here,
torn away from a gritty homeland
to bear twice their weight in gold,

to guard the sheep against the fox.
Not suited to wet or soft terrain
or leafy bush, danger of rain scald,

mud fever, they need a roof
or a raincoat belly-strapped
against squall, the fiber of furze

and barley straw, a farrier to fettle
their rotting hooves with pritchel,
and nipper, and rasp. In slanted shyness,

they rest their chins on the low wall
between us, human as we are
in their hunger for care and company.

Kris Feeds the Animals

She sorts our leavings into separate dishes.
        Some of them are carnivores, some, herbivores

She knows what time of day each one needs to eat
        and she knows where—uphill, under the sour sop tree,
        or on the dry grass by the stone wall

One goat eats the banana peels and onion skins
        and the other goat stacks them in a tidy pile

The two dogs remove all the fish bones delicately,
        the dog who belongs to a neighbor
        and the dog who isn't attached to anyone,

The chickens have pecked the yard to powder

The sheep bleating for her babies is tied to a tree and has
        grazed everything within reach

That sheep is patient as a deity, her eyes obsidian,
        carved, not polished

That sheep has nothing to do but wait

And Kris doesn't need them to look into her eyes
        She doesn't need them all to lick her hand

Ode to the Oysters

To the secret mollusks, not comely
but sufficient unto themselves—male
the first year, female after spawning,

and so on, back and forth, attaching
to each other by the thousands, building
reefs of themselves, cleaving to each other,

the living to the dead. To the farmer,
who fills fine-meshed cages first with oyster
seed, ties them to the dock, watches over them

for half a year as the tides do the washing
and feeding, culls the bigger spat into baskets,
anchors them in the pond to grow another half-year

until we make their acquaintance,
the clacking of shells, infinite variations
of grey, their beaten shapes, evidence

of a hard, slow, defenseless life, the piles alive
with the crawling and rolling of predators
who lurk in the baskets, like toadfish

and oyster drill, that tiny butcher. I sort
and count. The smallest ones, I load back
in the baskets for protection. Legals and almost-legals,

I cast upon the waters—life that will end with us,
the worst of the pillagers. And we so love
the primordial oyster, love the struggle to find

the insertion point, force the shell open,
taste the almost-living, briny-nakedness,
nexus of sex and the sea.

How to Become a Naturalist

From The Enquirer's Home Book, 1910
A Complete Guide For Every Branch Of Domestic Life

Don't collect plants when they're wet with dew.
Put dry ends in water to recover.
Heat a flat-iron and press them under a blotter.

Preservation has its rights and wrongs.
Never disturb a bird's nest.

Steep leaves in rain, leave them four months,
replenishing the rain-water.
With a small sable brush, remove
the epidermis and reveal the skeleton veins.

A creature should be in clear solution,
in a glass jar, tightly corked, succulent, peaceful.
A formula must be correct or it will harm the specimen.

After you chloroform a butterfly,
pin it to a setting-board through its thorax,
the iridescent wings outstretched.

Fish, too fragile for an amateur, give to a taxidermist.
My father's one and only prize, the biggest tuna caught in Miami,
he couldn't afford to mount, so he had the smaller tuna stuffed,
the one that didn't win, and it hung in my brother's
barn for years, eaten slowly by mice.

Three

Nor'easter, Salty Cottage

The house is lashed by storms.
The floors slant. The floor boards
buckle. The ceiling curves. The whole of it leans
toward the sea, yielding only as much as it needs to.

It is built to yield. The carpenter
does what he does and nature's
softening and bending
lets the house hold to rock.

The woman my friend once loved
had a cauldron boiling inside her,
like the sea outside this window,
a boiling she could not contain

and it destroyed all her self-regard.
Times I overheard her in the night—
her sounds were something other
than pleasure, something like this storm.

My Feet Are Planted on this Rock

Shopkeeper, Trinity Bay, Newfoundland

Nothing was easy. We searched deep and low
        for tiny fruit, marsh berries, ripe
                when frost spattered them gold.
                We dug into that stony soil

for our potatoes, hurried them into the root cellar.
        We named our outports Heart's Desire,
Chimney Tickle, Come By Chance.
        No roads, we traveled by dory in summer,

by dogsled in snow. Though we studied the thickness of ice,
        no one trusted our fishermen would make it back home
                to hole up for winter.
                Salt cod the mainstay of our table,

tea and sugar coming by occasional boat. We doctored ourselves
        with tinctures and rubs, schooled our children
                in mosses and puffins and murres,
                capelin at spawning-time,

and the children sailed their sleds giddy
        to the very edge of the world.
                Gleaning from that rock made everything sweeter.
                When great trawlers replaced our dories,
                factory fish plants our drying rooms,

and cod collapsed, we were forced off the rock, forced to leave
        that clear and blue and cold. Curtains blew through
                the open windows of the houses we left.
                Carrots shriveled in root cellars.

Some of us took our houses, floating them over the bay
    or hauling them over snow,
        two hundred men on the ropes,
          a job that took days, pulling inches at a time
          toward the city. The powers called it *resettlement*.

Water

Water flooding the streets, running off too soon

Too much of it for dikes and seawalls to hold back
We gamble against it; we gamble for it
We take our chances we won't drown
We take our chances we'll have enough
Water always has its way

Water we take for pleasure
Water we take for our lawn-grass
We take it to wash ourselves cleaner than clean
poison it with waste

River-dry, water-scarce, water-worry,
Water-lord says who can open up the head-gate,
let the watercourse fill
and when on the clock
and how long

We murder for water
Water is gold

A Small Caribbean Island with a Line from Auden

Dollar buses, names painted on the hoods
surfer-style—*Fear Not, Trust Me,* picking up

schoolgirls who squeal like sunshine reggae,
Rasta man slanging verses Marley-style,

for Marley is and always. Instrumental clack
of dominoes, and a drummer's steel brushes

hissing in the palms. Sudden rain on the metal roof
like gunshots. In the bush, someone's preaching

apocalypse and everywhere the animals
are rib-counting skinny, lambs who wandered off,

goats at the very end of their tethers,
stray dogs panting at our gate for any kitchen scraps,

and under the car, a terrible grinding mounts
the road so steep the concrete slabs shift tectonic.

We walk down to the waterfront
to buy barracuda steaks for the grill

. . . how everything turns away
Quite leisurely from the disaster . . .

Night Hisses Its Fast Downpour

An island keeps its own rapt counsel.
Seagrape reclaims the half-built hotels.
Drop one sweet rotting bean of the rosary vine

in the water and it could kill the village.
Sky turns brazen, a terrible radiance—
and the under voice, cruel, complicit,

nothing as it seems. Clouds take on the guise
of substance. Like the monkeys, you are scratching
for words, whether you speak or don't speak.

No god gives a tinker's dam.
You're in free fall, no toggle line,
no landing marker.

Which is heavier, a pound of potatoes
or a pound of grief?
Night hisses its fast downpour.

Turban your head in cloth
the color of squash blossoms.
One could wrap a corpse in such cloth.

The Green of Ireland

Green of Doolin, Sligo green.
Green of Carrowmore, Knocknarea,
      green that sails to Byzantium, proud and mythic.

Miscellany of green cartography, great green swathes.
Hornbeam, hazel, holly green against a broken sky.
Respectable, silent, muscular, hopeful green, innocent and
knowing.

Unpracticed ingenuous green that follows heart's desire.
Warm licking tongue of a green, incurably metaphorical.
Green of that place deep within fire.

Brazenly posturing, inexhaustible green.
Repressed green, falsely pious, fancy-talking, lying green.
      And the green of truth.

Green awakened from a nightmare.
Cloak of green covering ignorance.
Green of a journey, green of the home place.

Passionate green and a green that is slow unwinding.
Green that never admits to longing.
Green won't ride in on a horse to save you.

Green of love drifting away.
Spectacularly failing green.
Green of authority, green of injustice, green of revelation.

Famine and hunger, green of the dispossessed.
Green of ritual, of the Mass, the rosary.
Green of fairies, green of the loss of fairies.

Green of the curtain slowly opening.
Green staring out the window.

Independence

Taos, July 4th

We stand where other peoples stood
for thousands of years, their houses
rising from clay. The Blue Lake and the corn

they held sacred. Their unwritten language,
they called Tiwa, and they danced to the deer
and the buffalo, until we arrived.

Fire rages in the north, and we don't speak of it,
don't even think fire, the way villagers in Auschwitz
didn't think fire, though their gardens were covered in ash.

We the people read the Declaration, each of us
one paragraph: *we mutually pledge to each other our Lives,
our Fortunes and our sacred Honor* and we tell our stories,

everyone from somewhere else—*Vienna, Dublin,
Toronto, Mumbai, Taipei,* and pride swells in us—
how we came here for sanctuary, we came to be free,

until the last man speaks, says *Senegal,* says, *Mandinka,
my people were taken; my people were kidnapped,
came here as cargo, came here in chains.*

Southwestern

—more sky than any place has a right to,
show-off sky, show-off mountains
with gold on their peaks, and weather,
lightning in one spot,
bluer than blue over there.

And the ground, undiggable,
blowable sandy ground, dust-devil,
dust-storm ground, wrecked-earth ground.
And silver: olive-trees, silver bushes
trying their best to hold down
the ground, the powder too weak
to hold back the rocks.

And thin air and high air, too high
to sleep, too high to think.

And big. Scrub-jays, big beetles, big-eared jack-rabbits,
symphony of crickets,
rattlesnakes waiting.

Loud wind, loud hissing rain.

Adobe here, adobe there, house, church, pueblo,
earth-built, sun-baked, the first builder so right
the ways of building never changed.

And faith, healing faith, saints-faith,
planting-faith, harvest-faith,
faith in the pure rushing stream.

Ode to Cidering

Guilford, Vermont

From trees unpicked, un-lovely, un-named fruit
fallen in October's bluster, not Winesap,
not Northern Spy, but yellow-skinned,

blemish more than flesh. Flung on the tarp.
Everything sticky. Gathered into buckets,
even the wasps. Fruit, worms and all,

decanted into the wooden press that takes
the strength of two to work—you smash
the tubful with a wooden club. I lean hard

on the grinder lid and you turn the grinding wheel.
The pieces tumble into a loose-staved barrel
lined with cloth and you screw down

the pressing plate tight, tighter, and from
that mash and the pommace after,
comes the pour of pure amber

we drink straight away. And here's to
the aging of it, the bottling,
the hardening, the warmth it gives.

Four

Winter Never Came

From the train on the way to Philadelphia,
I saw ash over the city, particles of the thousands,
ash that wouldn't clear for weeks,

and when I made a stop at Penn Station,
late September, notices Xeroxed, hand written,
posted on temporary fences,

photos melting in rain, and families lingering, stunned.
From an apartment house roof on Lower Broadway,
I saw the all-night march of the bulldozers,

a dozen, lifting and pivoting, piling
and sifting, sifting—steel skeletons spiring the sky,
day and night undivided, and winter never came.

By March, the vernal pool formed, neon, not a natural green,
algae, and likely, the obligate species,
fairy shrimp and salamanders,

and in a neighborhood shop window, a man's white shirt
on a mannequin torso, an ash-covered shrine
to the unnamed, the undocumented, the unrecorded.

The Constant Stream

I watch the rally on the kitchen TV—screaming,
untrammeled, news blaring through the ether,

interrupt paying bills to listen to the constant stream.
People don't really want to blow each other up,

my husband says, and goes out to mow the grass,
weaving his way among the tupelos. *Yes they do,*

I say to myself, and pour a cup of coffee, wondering
what I should hide from the barbarians. My daughter,

I think, and her daughter, from ignorant mobs
who think heaven awaits. In winter, someone

tromped a swastika in the snow behind the junior high,
and just last week at high school basketball,

fans chanted: *You killed Jesus!* Nerve-jangled,
I start to watch "My Own Private Idaho," with

River Phoenix, one more gifted actor who thought
he'd change the world, flamed out too young.

I need to keep up with my usual consolations,
make my Nana's Russian cabbage soup, slow,

and savor every shred. Come to my table
for good sweet and sour, the only certitude.

Would Anything Have Been Different?

If the mothers held their boys,
held them in their laps and let them cry,
and the boys were consoled,
and went to school to learn verses of love,

if the boys were consoled by mothers who walked
about the village with their bodies un-swathed,
if the mothers went to work
in the markets and the offices

with their bodies unswathed, if the mothers could
speak freely and join their voices
with others, and be joyous
at the weddings of their daughters,

if they could be joyous, play the tambourine and dance,
and no wife was flogged and no wife was jailed, and no wife's
hand was cut off and no wife was stoned in the street,
would anything have been different?

The Burqa

His eyes, the topaz of far hills,
hers, deep-welled and speaking,
his, hopeless, hers, levantine, gleaming.
His kindness remarkably embarrassed.

His part in it: a candle, rice
in a clay bowl. Impossible, the divide.
Before the street starts snooping
with its dangerous occupations,

she slides from his bed,
tiptoes over his uniform,
sand-gray as the village,
his helmet, his body armor,

and fallen from his cargo pockets:
radio, cellphone, candies,
flashlight, bullets, diary, pen,
heaped on the floor like killing stones.

She hurries into jeans, cotton
shift, wraps a silk scarf shot with gold
low on her forehead to cover
every hair; she lifts the burqa

and it settles over her head,
its small threaded window,
and floats down over her body,
yards and yards of unassailable blue.

On his desk she leaves him a pomegranate.
She thinks he is sleeping; from the bed
his hand darts out, fingers graze her ankle
the way even one breath might disturb the air.

The Birds in Babylon

Jittery from the lapwings' racket,
he straps on his ammo belt;
babblers snipe from behind the dump
and on the roadside pond

a phalarope swims tight circles.
From the start, he's watched them,
everywhere, a paradise of birds—
in the ruins of the palace,

the moat, the wasted orchard,
birds, going on with their lives.
Strangely comforting, a crested lark
seems to escort his convoy

into the city—streets shudder,
the flames unearthly blue, and even here,
the birds—sparrow hawks ravage
the fresh kill; storks ride the thermals.

After he's made prisoners strip
and dance, applying the field guide
to debasement, he builds a nest box
carefully for the barn owl hiding

in the airshaft in the bunker,
according to plans he sent for—
the wood preserved
for endurance, a balcony, a sluice,

and he adds sawdust and straw—
the nesting bits, and hangs it up
with the entrance hole
facing away from the west

The Lost Children

Sent away by their mothers
with a little food, a schoolbook,
to walk seven miles, ten miles,
to the city, to the courtyard
of the hospital, or crowded
on a veranda under light,
or sleeping rough, one boy
under the shea butter tree,
one boy among many, under
the millet, covered with stalks,
children practicing camouflage,
so they won't be stolen to be soldiers,
to be porters and whores, and they sleep
among the termites who make sandhills
on their bodies until first light
touches everything with gold.

Pray for them. Oh, pray for Jean-Claude
and Abdalla. Pray now
for the hurricane boys who pick
their way shoeless with a chew
of sugar cane. Let them comfort
and groom each other, let them find
a place safe tonight, safe from gangs
who stone them, rob them,
a doorway to hold two of them
or three, space enough for the sticks
of their limbs, one boy's back
against the belly of another.
Lay them down long and dreamless.
Let them sleep.

Earthquake Artists

The spirits of the dead were turned loose,
wandering the hillsides, wandering
the neighborhoods, loose and making trouble,
every spirit in need of a place to rest where
mourners can pour rum or coffee over a grave,
have conversations, and so the earthquake artists—
survivors, orphaned and widowed, very young,
very old—have work to do, to gather pieces
from the wreckage of buildings, from mausoleums
crushed to rubble, from bones heaved up, from
a doorway collapsed where a woman stood
one half step from living, and the artists build
sculptures of the remains, crowd shantytown
alleyways with images, encrust the walls—a blue family
welded from car parts, a man carved from a truck tire,
his plumbing pipe arms reaching out, a bleached skull
mounted on a board, all painted, patina'd, joyful,
accusatory, solemn, terrible, beautiful.
The artists labor by day, labor by the light
of the sparks from their tools, sharing paints,
old matted brushes, one holding a metal scrap
for another to fuse, and they labor for no money,
no honor, the work urgent as water seeking
a crack to flood, 300,000 spirits demanding a host.

Migrating Ducks

Mallards in the harbor,
hundreds, in full mallard dress,
bobbing on the bay in formation,
iridescent in green helmets, breasts
spanking white. Such a day!
The leader at the apex suddenly
shifts direction, swimming fast
against the current, and the ranks
fall in behind, obedient, a line,
like soldiers among the pines
in Auschwitz, at ease in full Nazi
uniforms, epaulettes to show rank—
enlisted man, officer, and medals
for bravery. At the River Sola,
the women are eating blueberries,
laughing. The men sing *Trinklieder*
in unison and one plays accordion
beneath the sky they share with mallards,
and at night they take a cigarette
under the same winking stars.

A Polish Woman, About to Save a Jewish Child Hiding Under Her Church Pew, Hesitates

A child must be silent.
A child must eat everything on her plate.
I'll serve her boiled egg, linen on the table.
A child must be bathed every evening and her fingernails cleaned.
I'll be very strict.
In the morning I won't wake her. Best she sleep all day
while I'm at work,
must not part the curtains, look out.
Her hair is a dark tangled thicket.
I'll hide it under my robin's egg scarf.
If the neighbors corner me on the stairs,
my niece, I'll tell them, my sister is ill.
They want my apartment—a woman alone.
I'll buy her a sprigged nightgown.
Gretel, I'll call her, teach her to read.
What if someone hears her coughing?
I could put her in the broom closet with blankets, close the door.
Should someone inform.
Should the soldiers come.
I would tear open my blouse
even if they beat my face bloody,
even if they shave my head.
Could I find a nun to hide her?
Could we run away to Mount Zar?
I love Mount Zar, the vast eternity.
I could steal this child. I could make this child mine.
I will let a child comfort me
in snow, in snow.

Intimacy

Sobibor Concentration Camp, Poland, 1943

Sara knew exactly
how many lashes
Jakob took on his buttocks.
She counted in a low whisper
while Jakob shouted,
eins, zvei, drei! louder and louder,
until viciousness
was exhausted.
And it took eighteen thrusts
for the drunken guard
to spend himself in her,
fall away in stupor.
After the breakout,
in the hayfield where
they hid half a mile
from the gates,
Jakob held her,
just holding,
expecting nothing,
and Sara touched his wounds
as if touch alone could heal.

Keep Marching

Brookline Holocaust Witness Project

One day, the guards loaded
all the women and children
onto trucks. I thought
for a minute this was a kindness,
letting the women ride
while the men were forced to walk,
but the women and children
were driven to the gas chambers.
The guards ordered us to keep
marching. If we couldn't march,
they'd shoot us. We were starving.
Ahead of me in the line,
one man dropped. His brother
tried to help him up.
The guards shot both of them.
I started to fall to my knees
and then I said to myself,
I'm not going to die.
I'm much too young to die—
I wasn't even twenty—
and I straightened up
and marched on through fields
of clover. I knew clover
wasn't poisonous, so I ate it.
And I ate my belt.

Soldier

Fear bleached the sky bone-white, turned blood black
after war he will paint with charcoal
the imperative of war, paint
canvas after canvas blackened with ash

after war he will paint with charcoal—
ash, smeared and rubbed and scratched away
canvas after canvas blackened with ash.
Let him step back, step back to see what he's exhumed—

ash, smeared and rubbed and scratched away
carboned, sooty, smudged with work,
he steps back, steps back to see what he's exhumed—
the minimal, fused flanks of the near-dead

carboned, sooty, smudged with work:
prisoners hanging hollow, slight as sticks,
the minimal, fused flanks of the near-dead
and after war, he will not return to color

prisoners hanging hollow, slight as sticks—
the imperative of war, he will paint
after the war, and he will not return to color.
Fear bleached the sky bone-white, turned blood black

Five Ways of Spoons

In bed, my husband presses his belly
to my back. A man and a woman
and a spoon are two.
My son-in-law curves his huge builder's hand
to hold his baby's head.

And there are rules—for the serving dish,
a different spoon. If the table is formal,
and the spoons line up like accusers, work
from the outside in. Be of three minds,
though one isn't, really: soup, sorbet, dessert.

A spoon sits on my windowsill
washed up at low tide,
its patina ancient green,
scratched and rusted
from tarnishing the years.

A spoon is so often involved.
Jewish prisoners, forced to shovel
their dead into mass graves,
scrape their escape, spoonful by spoonful,
all night, months of nights, crawling.
Dawns, they bury their spoons in the dirt, indecipherable.

Five

The Application of Luck

Luck is a fact just as the winds and the tides are
—W. Lock Wei, 1925, *The Theory of Mah Jong*

Start with the sound of sparrows clattering.
Build a wall, break it, deal, discard,
laughing, shift your tiles to the South.

I thought you had luck.
You shone with Earthly Grace,
got the Moon from the Bottom of the Sea,
the Four Blessings at your Door.

I should have warned you
to be satisfied with small hands,
not to let a single chance of hazard
aggravate ill luck.
Yours turned down so fast
I was afraid for myself.

To Swim with Dolphins

She wanted that,
all summer in the hospital,

a pod of machines sounding her,
pumping in, sucking out,
her legs faint ripples in the sheets.

She loved to sail
to the eye of the wind, close-hauled,
taunting the rip-tide,
rolling with any wave who'd have her,
reduced to this puny adventure.

I stare at the city turned cadmium orange,
and wish she'd leave like sunset,
incendiary, streaks of fire her wake.

On Good Friday

My friend leans on the sea wall in pain, watching Jesus
drag the hand-hewn cross through Esperanza

but she is first to dive off
the little hired boat

into darkest water. Millions
of stars trail her, phosphorescent.

Bald, in her ivory swimsuit,
tiny stars tumble from her,

slide off her skin. I'll remember her
like this, spilling stars.

The Reign of Her Dying

Sometimes I simply sat with her
and rubbed her parchment feet.
Dying was imperious,
the hyperbole of it, the smell and utter quiet of it.
I needed it to be finished.
I wanted it to go on.

Death stripped her legs
and buttocks, ratcheted her down to bone.
Winter milked her eyes over.

Her beauty had been windblown
with a constancy of pearls,
a beach rose too thorny to hold,
and like plants abandoned, she praised me
and left me dry, praise she let out
the way a cheese-maker starts
with sweet, then sours and curdles it—
love and reprimand mingled.

Sweetie, Sweetie

Dead, you aren't pretty,
naked, ruined beneath the quilt,
skin like laundry on a drying rack.

Your eyes won't close,
your cheeks concave,
I can't talk about your breasts.
Your belly's slumped
but your feet are alabaster,
beautiful and strange,
each toe a little plumped-up pillow.

Each of us greets you—
dry, warm, unresisting,
thin as a parachute,
downed and settling slowly.
We dampen napkins
in a basin, stroke your arms, legs,
rub your chest,

pour tiny pools of oil
into each other's palms
and crooning to you,
shine your body.

Part by part, we shroud you,
bodice, bib for your throat, tunic,
all ravel-edged, homespun, square,
tie the headpiece under your chin,
cloak your swollen white hands,
pull on the trousers, the bottoms sewn shut,
one, two, three, together lift
the heavy sum of weightlessness.

Oh, Sweetie, sweetie,
we are trembling,
the closest we've ever been to you
and you aren't here.

Midwife

Also, healer. Mucker, milker, weaver, gardener,
baker, mother, wife. She keeps a diary
of passion and misery—the man who drags
the coffin of his wife past mounds
of mussel shells to open water,

and murder—a farmer sharpens his flensing-knife,
cuts his wife in her bed, six children, takes
a razor to his own throat. The corpses she washes,
lays them in the barn according to their ages,
the farmer interred outside the churchyard wall.

and birth—the mistress crouches like a cat near the fire,
calls the neighbor-wives to hold her, breathe her quick rhythms,
her grunts. She yells curses on her mother, expels
that mottled thing. The midwife catches it, wipes it till it pinks—
takes her fee, six shillings, in coffee and cod.

Black Hitty comes up from Jamaica when the birches
are bare as prison bars, tears the tie off her apron,
lifts up her shift, scent of his skin on her bedclothes—
the hemlocks shiver like royal palms and when
that baby comes, it shines like an aubergine.

To the Captain's wife she's called, who throws herself
upon the sea of birth, the slump of it, the place where one
might cease to be. Nature does it in her own sweet time.
Nothing to nothing, and in between, a daughter,
with eyes of their own charitable depths.

She keeps a tally of the living:
eight hundred and fourteen born, one hundred and six
first births, forty out of wedlock, two unexplained,
keeps a tally of the river,
when it ices over, when it breaks.

Refugees

        neither prophecy nor flicker—
the crowd in the rank oily air, in the dusk and dim
      and swirling steam
           of the bus station, kids
in leather, in white-white sneakers,
      the girls' lips redder and plumper than a billboard ad,

      and the boys who circle in baggy jeans so low
          it takes a wide rolling gait to keep them up,
    some jittery, some drugged or hallucinating,
declaiming an apocalypse to the big-eyed baby in his stroller,
      and swearing fast in a stew of Spanish-English,
a girl chewing gum furiously and another girl with another baby,

          and a boy or is it a girl in a too-huge black hoodie
              down to the knees, with a skeleton on it,
        front and back—parades up to the other kids
            who pay no attention, the head
      so deep inside you can't see the face—

and the two girl-mamas kiss full on the lips, long enough
         for the world to drop away,
              for the film to stutter and flare,
                    for the boys to go still.

Citizenship

*An applicant for naturalization must demonstrate
that he or she is of good moral character.*

A quiet multitude awaits my help, though
twenty pages can't tell who they really are:
the man who can fix a washing machine
with baling wire, the woman who reproduces

any dress with her foot-pedaled machine.
Just the facts: birthdates of children,
alive, dead, missing, spouses and current
spouse's prior spouses. Francois says

his children's mother has no address.
On that line, I write Haiti. Where
have you been working and living?
Five years' worth. And offenses the INS suspects.

Are you a Nazi, Commie, military, paramilitary,
vigilante, guerrilla, drunkard? Do you use
racial epithets? Do you incite hate crimes?
Have you ever badly hurt a person? On purpose?

Have you ever groped someone's private parts?
Paid hush money? Ever sold yourself for sex acts?
Which ones? Do you have more than one wife?
How many? Is your income from illegal gambling?

Did you falsify your passport? Eduardo's police report
shows he did, to bring a new baby with him.
Did you lie on your tax returns or fail to file
your taxes? Did you ever steal food?

The correct answer is no.
If you lie when you answer no, you may be deported.
If you answer yes, you may be deported.

Toehold

Every day you make the choice
to live on the slippery ledge,
where you almost always fail
to find a toehold, mesmerized
by the gelid clarity of water
or the far-off blow
of blue-green radiance,
the steely whistle
of work and money,
the softer mist of love,
everything draws you—
the cold burn seizing
anyone who stands up
in the boat. Paddle through
the irresistible archway.
Take a piece of the iceberg
to chill your cocktail.
It can roll over you.
Virtue will carry you
only so far and help
never comes fast enough.

Random Music

Poetry's a risky inclination.
Sentiment can smother all my lines
when I let nostalgia take the place of beauty
so I ignore the bunnies on the planter-full of pansies.
The news only gives me novel ways to die.

I go out to the marsh, search for random music—
the opening of barnacles as the tide retreats,
study the parable of stars in their dumbshow,
the curtain of dawn unfurling, baring this day
of lonely sameness—walk, write, cook, eat.

Life's lonely sameness—cook, eat, write, walk,
the curtain of dawn unfurling, baring this day.
Study the parable of stars in their dumbshow,
the opening of barnacles as the tide retreats,
and out at the marsh, search for random music.

The news gives you unconscionable ways to die.
Ignore the bunnies on the planter-full of pansies.
Don't let nostalgia take the place of beauty,
or sentiment will smother all your lines.
Poetry's a risky inclination.

About the Author

Margot Wizansky's chapbook, *Wild for Life,* a chronicle in poems of her near-death and the coma that followed, was published by Lily Poetry Review Books (2022). *The Yellow Sweater,* a full-length poetry collection, was published by Kelsay Books (2023).

Her poems have appeared online and in many journals such as *The American Journal of Poetry, The Missouri Review, Bellevue Literary Review, Ruminate, River Styx, Cimarron,* and elsewhere. She edited the anthologies *Mercy of Tides: Poems for a Beach House* and *Rough Places Plain: Poems of the Mountains* and co-edited *What the Poem Knows: A Tribute to Barbara Helfgott Hyett.*

She was awarded two residencies, one with Writers@Work in Salt Lake City and one with Carlow University in Sligo, Ireland at the Isle of Innisfree. Margot has retired from a career developing housing for adults with disabilities. She lives in Massachusetts.

www.ingramcontent.com/pod-product-compliance
Lightning Source LLC
Chambersburg PA
CBHW030909170426
43193CB00009BA/795